It Would Be Quiet

Jan LaPerle

Copyright © 2013 Jan LaPerle

All rights reserved.

Published in 2013 by Prime Mincer Press

ISBN-10: 0988296101
ISBN-13: 978-0988296107

CONTENTS

Section One: Adventure, Adventure
She Rings Like a Bell Through the Night, 3
All Of Them Taking Flight At Once, 6
Fiddle, 7
Pluto, 8
Stitch, 9
One Day Soon, 11
Motherhood, 14
Station Attendant, 15
My Father's Campers, 16
Beautiful Surfaces, 19
Shower Cap, 21
Pretty Rooster, 22
Rain On Administrative Professionals Day, 23
Costume Girl, 24
Spider, 25
Bulb Under Snow, 26
Winter Gossamers, 27
The Midwife, 28
Winter Wedding Waiting, 29

Section Two: Or Sit By the Door
The Sweetness (No, The Sadness) Of A Summer Storm, 33
Killing Him Didn't Make the Love Go Away, 35
Tractor Race, 37
Lumber, 38
New Motorcycle, 40
Adventure, Adventure, Or Sit By the Door, 42
The Roof, 43
The Sisters, 45
House, 46
Letter After the Circus, 47
Frost, 48
Even the Radio, 49
Saturday Afternoon Remodeling the Camper, 50
I Touched Her Hand and It Felt Like Snow, 51
Valentine's Day, 53
Wintering, 54
The Weight and Washing Up, 55
It Would Be Quiet, 58

ACKNOWLEDGMENTS

"The Weight and Washing Up" *The Cape Rock* 40.1 (2012): 22-23

"Killing Him Didn't Make the Love Go Away" and "One Day Soon This Is All Gonna End, One day Soon Maybe It'll All Begin: For Me and My Washing Machine" *Shadowbox* 4 (2012): online

"Pluto" *Gargoyle Magazine* 58 (2012): online

"Stitch," "New Motorcycle," and "Adventure, Adventure Or Sit By the Door" *Prime Mincer* (2012): 62,63

"She Rings Like a Bell Through the Night" *Rattle* 35 (2011): 33

"Lumber," "Costume Girl," "Frost," and "Winter Wedding Waiting" *Blazevox* 2KX (2010): online

"My Father's Campers" *Quicksilver* 1 (2009): online

"Letter After the Circus" *42Opus* 9 (2009): online

"Tractor Race" *Boxcar Poetry Review* 17 (2008): online.

"Motherhood" *Subtropics* 5 (2008): 26.

"Arbor Day" and "I Touched Her Hand and it Felt Like Snow" *Illya's Honey* 14
(2008): 94, 96.

"The Sisters" *West Wind Review* 26 (2007): 3.

"Even the Radio" and "The Roof" *The Heartland Review* 7 (2007): 11, 46.

"House" *Tar River Poetry* 46 (2006): 32.

Part One:

Adventure, Adventure

All I want to do is stay awake, keep my head up, prop my eyes open, with toothpicks, with trees.
— Annie Dillard

SHE RINGS LIKE A BELL THROUGH THE NIGHT

Yesterday my husband bought a Lincoln Town Car.
As we were driving to pick it up he said how it was once
the longest car in America. Sometimes I don't have to imagine
what he'll be like when he's old. I can see,
clearly, tonight, the moon.

                To the moon and back
is how I love you, I said, and what I say now
to my month-old daughter. But that's not right;
that's not enough. To the moon and back and back and back
when I was first getting to know my husband I lied,
told him I only wanted to be friends. I remember his eyes,
a ship through ice.

Ship-fronts scare me, and that is what I felt like pregnant —
so big and capable of so much: so much good; so much bad.
It was the bad I dwelled on. I watched videos of babies
with two heads, many legs, nothing at all for eyes.
I was sure I was ruining her, somehow, someway:
the fluffernutter, too many tuna fish sandwiches.

I thought once I gave birth I'd be relieved if she was okay.
I could sleep through the night and stop dreaming of her
sleeping in my arms, a pole for a head.

One fear replaces another. Each night now I wake
in fear that I've crushed her in bed. Sometimes it's so bad
I wake the husband and the two of us, in the slight light
of the streetlight, are in there, in the king bed digging,
through pillows and sheets, looking for our baby.
Digging and digging as if our bed was the terrible ground
beneath the floorboards. We sweat, breath heavy;
I'm crying.

The power to kill something is so strong up in me,
and so strange to be right next to the part of me
that can love something this much. It's the sort of love
I want to tell people without children about,
as mothers and fathers once told me. But this is impossible.

And it's impossible to think of my life before her
(as they said it would be) – to think of how it was when
I first saw my husband, how I imagined our life together
even then, even when he was someone else's.

How quickly life can change direction. I wonder
if all couples imagine their husbands or wives old,
themselves old. I wonder if my parents had done so
when they were first married, decades before their divorce.
They couldn't have known where their lives were going.
I wonder about the ease of a U-turn in our Lincoln Town Car.
A U-turn over the highway median: illegal. Sad.

I do not want my husband to leave me.

There are so many fears in me. When I try to fall
asleep I can hear a knocking against the headboard.
Someone is already at my door with the big, bad news.
So I sleep for a little while until the baby wakes me.
Sometimes I'm so tired when she wakes I get
so damn mad at her. Last night I set her
little screaming body on the countertop,
simple, like a set of keys. Her little hand was hitting
against the lever on the toaster. I think now it might
have looked like she was making toast. She had to hit
against something to wake me, to tell me
I was being a bad mother, selfish for wanting sleep
more than wanting to care for her, her little belly
empty as the streets (terrible when they're empty).

The lake sits at the end of our street.
The sad boats float. One going this way, one that –
that's how I see our marriage going sometimes.

As if our love will turn into something obligatory —
something to maintain like the lawn,
or a loosening shutter.

          Something in me is loosening.
I dream each night of flying. Once, years ago,
I pranked my father, told him his house in Florida
had been hit by a storm. Pieces of his house were loosening.
I disguised my voice, made it old and cranky. The funniest part
is that he believed this voice.

Inside of me is the old fuddy-duddy I will someday be.
I feel her in there, like a pregnancy. Aren't there so many
parts of us? Young, old, our children, parents.
Luckily, now, we have a big car — it stretches
across our driveway, ready to hold us, like a big, big hand.

ALL OF THEM TAKING FLIGHT AT ONCE

This is the 35th time in my life I have felt the spring,
but the first time I have spent the season
teaching a little girl, my little girl, the names for things.

Yesterday: ear. This morning: balloon,
her favorite thing in the world. In a story I read last night
a man stole a hot air balloon from his neighbor.

He floated above his house, his yard where his wife and son
stood waving. Such a warm story, their faces glowing
in the sunshine, their little hopes pretty as the leaves.

The balloon and basket scraped against the branches
as it lifted higher and higher and higher. Then, the man jumped.
He jumped into the yard where his wife and son stood waving.

I do not know what the man's family felt right then.
When I try to understand I think only of a field
of geese, all of them taking flight at once.

A pause at the stop sign: I cannot see over the knoll.
My daughter in the back seat kicking her feet.
Our dog beside her wishing for a run in the graveyard.

A family I had once known said goodnight to their three-
year old son and in the morning, while a cardinal fed at their feeder,
they found him in his bed, blue as a pretty spring sky (how dare I

call it pretty). I hang clothes on the line. The shadows
of the socks stand in the grasses around me. These ghosts,
I am making them – I do not want to, but I cannot stop doing this.

FIDDLE

I bought my mother binoculars for Mother's Day so she can watch
the birds: blackbirds, white birds, and I've been using them.

I look deep into the trees. I watch the neighbor fall asleep
in his porch swing, roll this way, roll that, a black bag at his feet.

Knowing him, he's been collecting things, cookies or grief (oh,
how everything flies). It's really too far to see anything.

When a little girl down the street tightened her little fist,
I felt she'd closed it inside mine. We are not close,

but in the sweet spirit of my mother's binoculars, I've been trying.
I told the deli-man at the supermarket I'm going to be a wife.

He told it to the knife. The knife cut the meat, butcher block,
counter top, spoons, forks, tiles on the floor: the grocery store split

into hemispheres. As I stood by the cheese I watched my man
walk away from me. It seems too simple to need peanut butter.

Sometimes I try to forget my face. Sometimes when I wake
I catch the night fly off. Black bird in the tree. I look

through my mother's binoculars. I watch my man dream, inside it:
our house, the shutters tightly holding on. He dreams of our
wedding

replayed in different settings. Rain, snow, sunny morning,
and a white bird flies across the sky in a hemisphere still so black.

PLUTO

The widow next door is not going to change
her mind about the planets today, or the leaves,
or how each leaf has a spirit, she thinks,
and when she stands naked at the window
shadows of leaves fall across her: I mistake her,
again, for a symbol – for dying, the dead.
I saw in her a message from the trees,
and how fog is not fog at all, but the spirits of leaves –
they haunt and they hunt. The genocide of trees.
Hear her: Do the haunts love? Do they weep for me?
Dew is not dew at all, and she is not a tree,
and we figure some by what they are not.
She is not you or I so we do not need to love her,
but tell me: is Pluto a planet or not?
Tell me more about her, tell me before the wind stops,
before the leaves stop swimming across her, before
the last bowl is cleaned of its soup and spoon.
And I am talking to the leaves again.
I am talking to the last leaf on a far tree, a real holder-on.
The last leaf holds at the branch-tip. The last leaf
seems nervous, and I think the widow is watching.
Does she know what it is holding for?
The tattered flag whips. The garbage can rolls to the road.
A nest in the high branches is no longer a secret.
The widow and I know, no matter what they say
about Pluto, no matter what they say about trees,
we can think whatever we want about the last leaf.

STITCH

Sometimes, when I think of the Austrian daughter kept prisoner in the basement
by her father, I wonder if she learned to knit. Or, like me, if she preferred the stitch of

crochet —
a looser stitch, a lot like the pattern of a net. I wonder what *she*
would catch. Catch, catch, catch me if you can, I say when I let her
free, when I let her run in the garden
with me. When she brushes against the flowering trees, blossoms fall,
and where they fall in the grasses the ground blooms — a pregnant ground,
a pregnant girl, and the babies move in her like candy & fruit.
I almost know she knits for those little melon heads with stitches
tight as a noose.
Their cries are little songs: the only sound she hears from the outside
world is that of the
locomotive!
I, too, hear the train from here as I slowly crochet a scarf, a net for
my neck, strings strung like a rope. I read yesterday about a war in
China, how the men-soldiers strung
the naked women together by their necks like caught fish. I imagined their skin
in the sun glistening like fish. I hated to think they were so beautiful that way,
and I went to them on accident in the fog of a long gray dream dressed in my new sex,
where I moved through them like a locomotive.

Even in my dreams I feel guilty. But, still, they were only girls on paper: paper dolls
to slip over like a paper dress. And all at once they were pregnant.
When I pulled my hair from its pins it fell like water to the floor,
and splashed in a pool like a skirt. I, too, was pregnant then, but when I walked from my
 dream
I set down my pregnancy like a bag of groceries and woke: flat belly, flat, flat chest,
and my man behind me reaches with his big, big hands
for the big breasts of her ghost.

All these women are real to me. I catch them stitch-by-stitch. Lately I've begun to feel
their hair, corn silk between my fingers. Corn, corn, these women smell like corn,
and I eat them like a wild pig on the cob.

ONE DAY SOON THIS IS ALL GONNA END
ONE DAY SOON MAYBE IT'LL ALL BEGIN:
FOR ME AND MY WASHING MACHINE

Bleach

Even in the mornings, my baby's breath is clean as a sheet.
At the supermarket last night a little girl, maybe ten years old,
had her whole face planted inside a lily. She stood there for so long,
taking it in. It's not often enough that I stand against pretty things
and breath. We wake with breath more awful than the rubbish.
The dog yawns wide as a crane straight from licking his nasty rump.
I am too domestic these days, I tell my husband, I'm too boring.
The washing machine spins in the basement, and I too am down
there
like an animal in its hole drudging away, drudging away.
I wake in the mornings, heavy with a dream of my father
with hair (he's bald as the sun). The dream slips. In slippers,
I move toward the ironing board. My husband says I should
spend less time cleaning. While he was cooking mussels last night,
he dripped butter on the floor, dropped onion, the garlic's little white
coat.
When he wasn't looking I got down on my hands and knees
with my bleached cloth (I am a goddamned cleaning machine!)
and scrubbed those dirty tiles till they were stupidly clean.

Sheets

We were on a highway traveling south. A car in the north-
bound lane was speeding along with a mattress strapped to its top,
the whole front end of which was lifted in the wind.
My husband and I thought this to be hilarious.
We find the same things to be funny – such a small thing.
Small things magnify in a glass, small things rattle in our cupboards,
our cupboards that are filled and I just keep adding more,
emptying the dishwasher early in the morning, loudly
so the husband will wake, rise from our king-sized mattress

only so I can rush up and make the bed, sweep the sheets clean
of our little foot-droppings, our hairs. I don't like the dog
on the furniture, but my husband does (we discuss this
as I pull a cup from our cupboard). I don't like how on a sunny day
you can see the dust spinning around in the air, but my baby
does – she reaches for it, comes away with nothing.
She is not yet programmed for this type of disappointment.
The lilies I transplanted are drooping; I have done them wrong.

Dirt

A few days ago I read a poem about an elderly couple
who decided to take their lives together. They left milk
for their cats. The snow filled the cornrows.
My baby recently weaned herself and I feel both relieved
and terribly unwanted. We buy milk at the supermarket,
and there we see elderly couples walking together.
I say to my husband, that is us. When I read that poem I thought,
that is us. When I look at my little girl I think,
who is she, this girl that talks in little noises, this girl
that prefers drawer handles and door hinges to toys.
This girl that reaches happily for dust. We recently moved
into this house. The flowers blossoming in our yard are surprises
left for us. Our house that was a foreclosure; our house that is
haunted
by the sadness of having to leave a place before the spring
comes with her flowers from the bulbs
you (who are you?) had planted years and years and years before.
I've known my husband for less than five years,
but I'd go to the dirt with him – I'd lay there and sleep,
forever there. In the graveyard where I bring our dog
to run, someone planted daffodils the whole length
of the coffin beneath. I roll the stroller to the edge
of the patch so my baby can take it all in.
I photograph the dog running happily between
the tombstones. I submit this photo to the pet
photo contest at the supermarket. I cross my fingers.

Clothespin

For years I've been asking my husband for a clothesline.
I do not understand how the outdoors can seem so cleansing
yet when the outdoors comes indoors the indoors
then feels so dirty. I wipe the dog's paws with a cloth.
I bleach the cloth. I fold the cloth. I put the cloth
into its designated drawer. My baby watches me
from the sidelines. Today, when she was supposed to be
napping, I found her trying to climb out of her crib,
climb up the wall like a beetle and I automatically wondered
if she's trying to get away from here, away from me.
In the dream about my father with hair I can't decide
if he was a younger version of himself or if I was worrying
about the genes I'm passing on, the little surprises waiting
beneath the surface of my daughter. My daughter, she blossoms.
I fade and flatten, grow more scared and cynical and bored.
She delights at her image in the mirror. I am jealous of her,
her fresh start, her beauty as clean and real as the dogwood
bursting outside the window. My husband tells me
exactly how he will build that clothesline, the materials
he will use, but he does not build it. He remodels
the kitchen, the bathrooms, paints the walls, builds a deck.
Maybe he already hears, too loudly, the whipping
of the sheets, smells the sun burning the bleach,
sees his wife standing in the dirt, between the pillowcases,
lifting and pinning, lifting and pinning and waiting and waiting
and waiting.

MOTHERHOOD

The babies in my dream,
tiny as thumbs, hung
from little metal hooks
at the supermarket.
Simple as jars, they were,
and so was my decision
to take them, cradle them
like a child with the fresh apples
of a low orchard branch.
The babies were so little,
I might have swallowed them.

Now they grow in me,
ready to explode with the secret
force of spider eggs.
The eggs behind my mother's toilet
that rolled out from underneath
the mother spider like a pocket
pulled from a pair of jeans.
My mother told me how that spider
pushes her little legs out over
her eggs to protect them.
What a good mother,
I said, and she thought
I was speaking of the spider.

STATION ATTENDANT

Several days ago we drove the long way home,
road dust following behind us, over shadows of fence posts
asleep on the road. The neighbor's house crept into view
as we mounted the knoll. I noticed a clothesline,
and the clothes, from that far off, looked like blossomings.
(It is spring, and I've been looking hard.)

It is spring, and the neighbor is often in the yard
with his tractor, as he was a few nights ago.
The neighbor is a train conductor, and, once, years ago,
when my husband and I were there for dinner,
I told the train conductor that I thought his job
was romantic. The train conductor laughed.
His wife chewed her meat as he told me about
the things he hauled, the length and speed of his train.

My husband and I were taking the long way home
because, he said, we had to talk. Beyond city limits,
we traveled the square tiles of section lines.
East, north, west, south, and you can get yourself
back to where you began. The sun is too bright sometimes
to talk, the spring too good for bad news.

Beside that old tractor, the train conductor told us
how his son had filled the dryer hose with water.
The small hole on the side of the house
had seemed to the little boy like a tank, and he,
for a while, was the station attendant.
How early boys learn to pretend, I thought,
as I watched my husband blink into the sun.

MY FATHER'S CAMPERS

My father's campers are parked in a row along the barn.
Four of them and he lives in them all. Yes, all. One for the toilet,
shower – a little slide of the soap in, let's say, the hygiene camper.
The camper pulled up into the barn shadows is for sleeping.
A third for cooking – a little luncheon on wheels, though the wheels
never turn. The longest, newest, shiniest camper with the magnificent
awning that yawns out over a set of crooked lawn chairs is, what we shall
call, the socializing camper. In the humidity, the scrabble board wilts,
just a little.

        A little disjointed house. Imagine, now, the makings of a good
earthquake. Or rooms that could not get along. Children pulled apart
and sent to their rooms. The divorce of bedrooms. Children grow,
move across town, build more children, add bedrooms, bedrooms onto
bedrooms and bedrooms we never build into.

I'd like to keep this image from you:
father moving between rooms in the sunshine – a glint of light on his bald,
bald head. At night, stars reflected in his glasses. And other things
I'd turn you from or show you then say, Let's go. Go, go, go
as we all must do. Leaving a part of us as we go
like when father drives his bathroom down the yard,
toward town, toward another state and country and we don't think
of the happiness of the bathroom, but of the longing of the three campers
left against the barn.

          Lately, as I empathize with campers,
I consider how love is like a cartoon. A funny, on-the-page
sort of thing that isn't quite real, yet something I follow,
aimlessly, like a road and as I move toward one town,
I move away from another. From one room to another,
I wonder if the hygiene camper (at the mercy of its driver)
contemplates whether it can do without the other rooms
as I must do without you.

I tell you, I'd forever sleep in a tub for you. I'd do a lot of things.
Sometimes you have to do without as you do with what you have
and what you have to do. Like when my brother, shopping
with a hungry baby had to pull a jug of milk right off the shelf
and the baby, not knowing how to drink, but hungry, so, so hungry still
had to sit in his little spill. Of course he cried like we all cry
when no one knows why and maybe we do or don't know why or what for,
but that we are all hungry. The sleep camper cries for the hygiene camper.
I cry for the man because looking at him is like looking
at the sun and my brother's wife cries because the babies won't stop
crying or because the babies grow up right there behind the groceries
and I grow and wonder where my babies are. And the barn,
that big, big barn beyond the campers cries for us all.

        And why not consider crying babies? The daycare across
the street sends theirs off in a long stroller – a baby train.
Or they walk the babies chained together – a baby chain gang –
and they learn early the drudgery of following another
so closely you don't even know if you are you or just an extension
of someone else. An engine in a machine that could not run without you.
What good are you without that body? And I say,
why don't you rev up in mine.

Oh, I know very well that some of us are just meant to park.
The cooking camper, for instance, with its motor turned down,
its underneaths set up on blocks, knows how a little domesticity

will keep it alive — a stir of soup, a link of sausage
rolls in its pan — how quiet images of happiness are sometimes
enough.
But when hygiene camper returns, rolls in, sputters off,
full of road stories and sweat, the others grow scared.
Scared of their own stagnancies. Scared of everything, then,
scared, even, of the barn and the barn grows scared of the sun,
the sun the stars, the stars the campers, the campers the wilting
scrabble board, and the wilting scrabble board grows scared
of its players who press down with their eager little fingers
their little letters then sing out their little words and their little
points (oh, their points!) like they really are getting the point
or that they really have words for any of this.

BEAUTIFUL SURFACES

A pulled shade: a dirty window and what is left to think?
Dirty.

Dirty, dirty, dirty and a lone truck rumbles,
exhales into the yard between us. I beg from my little spot:
leave, truck, go, pick up your load.

I watch the trucker who seems more like a man
and I love her for that. She is not dedicated to the terrible
art of being a woman. I mean,
I dreamed last night of getting my eyebrows waxed,
contemplated a pedicure with the carefulness
of a senator with his papers.
What is left to think but that I am more a waste
than the black puffs let up from the truck?

And as the truck blackens the sky
I think of my night: black, silent, solitary,
no different than death and now I have to say:
read this without pity: the black of night
is perfect: my trophy: a stellar gift at the end
of a long movement through a sorry set of translucencies.

The truck – dusty and real – is so alive!
        But the truck does not leave,
just rumbles from its spot. Has the trucker
fallen asleep behind the monstrosity of her wheel?
I met the trucker once by the mailbox.
We watched the child next door play with his balloon.
Oddly, she explained to me how she,
being a very large woman, must heave
herself from bed and how she often
falls to the floor with a thud.

What is left to think of but the ladies in the apartment
beneath hers, how they must, from behind their teacups, groan
at the sound of the trucker's fall. Little indifferent puffs
rise between the ladies into the cold morning. Lipstick
swirls atop their tea like oil on the ocean: beautiful surfaces —
        quite unlike my dirty window. Yet,

if I were to live in a row of houses —
    houses docked like harbor boats — instead of next to
this truck lot, I would not witness such productive movements —
to the mill. To the builders building!   And watching the truck,
in all its stir, rumble around the corner
fills me with the optimism normally reserved
for a child. A child like the one next door who, that afternoon,
released his balloon into the sky with such fearlessness and joy.

SHOWER CAP

When I napped under a tree, fruits and vegetables grew
from my feet. Every time I wake the lines beneath my eyes
have grown deeper. Oh, okay, good morning. Oh rooster,
cock-a-doodle-do. I love you, too, but tell me, when I stand
among the pretty fruits do I look a little like a weed?
I'm sad today so hold me. I'm sad that my pretty dress
is at the alteration shop, the seamstress with fingers like pins.
I keep the door unlocked at night in case that dress
like an old scared dog comes back to me. I need that dress;
I need to look pretty, like a fruit. I tend to the rows with a hoe.
Vegetables at my feet. Creases in the dirt, and in my face
where the waters have run. The bugs have run. Run rooster run:
the dog is hungry. I am hungry for pie. Blueberry, blackberry,
and this afternoon I will paint my fingernails peach.
When I hold them out to you, will you eat them?

PRETTY ROOSTER

No matter where I walk in this town I can hear the rooster crow.
He says what he wants, whenever he wants. The wild rabbits run
full speed over the road, and everyday I see myself aging.

Everyday I see the woman up the road. She is beautiful,
has legs like steamboats, and when she throws them over the porch-
edge, her son swings from them. She waves when I walk past.

Weeks ago, when the peonies were in full bloom, her son's head
was deep in a bush of them, sniffing. *Momma, these flowers smell
like your bosom,* he said. Children and roosters have something on me.

I stop and look (but even this I'm overly conscious of)
how the bony trees of winter are filling out, leaf-by-leaf,
thicker and thicker. I am trying my damndest to do the opposite.

Once, in the woods, I found a shard of glass, and beside it,
the shed skin of a snake. The robins peck in the turned dirt
of a garden. I tried on a dress, pulled it off. I am hungry

for something I cannot put my finger on. I walk through the grave-
yard. People come with their terrible flowers, stay just a minute.
I stay for a long time. Beside a few headstones, peonies grow.

Mrs. Oliver, I say, *Emma, these flowers smell lovely.* So she'll know,
so she'll remember. Maybe she can't even hear me. Sometimes I
hear
myself and I hate what I'm saying, but I keep speaking anyway.

I do not know what my bosom smells like. I do not know if I will
ever
have a son, or if the peonies will remind anyone ever again of that
thing
inside us (that thing I can't put my finger on), growing, budding,
blossoming.

RAIN ON ADMINISTRATIVE PROFESSIONALS DAY

This, my dear, could have been a great day for an office job.
My chair has wheels, and a sense of easy moving
enters my mood (a mood I could not otherwise get to).
I am a woman of businesses. My tattoo, hidden
under my sock, blooms inside my shoe for you.
For you! For you! I yell out across the office for you.
But, who's who? Whose donut is whose? They all stare
at me, and when I kiss each one, each time,
donut and I become a redundancy of sweet mouths.
Sweet fingers, a little sweetness on this document
for you, then you, then you. Label, stamp, envelope,
a woman on wheels, and look how easily everything moves.
Roll, turn, roll, turn, staples, papers, and clips –
if this is the orgy of professionals (this thing I recognize
all around me, this thing too busy to say hello to),
and I, too, have become just another,
fattening in the stack for you, I'll brave the rain,
a punch out, a quiet adieu.

COSTUME GIRL

My life is more interested in windows this morning,
and I love deeply the fences between our houses.
This is the type of day the moon sticks around.
Hello, moon, I say, you are truly my friend today.
You listen to me and that's all I ever really wanted,
all I will ever need, my dear. Oh dear.
Oh dear, I love you, moon. Oh dear, love me.
Oh dear, the church bells are telling me the time,
telling me it is a day to go out into,
despite the sad pumpkins, despite the rotten pumpkins,
smashed pumpkins, despite, despite, a little spite, too,
but this isn't the saddest day, not even close,
but sadness is all around – lurking,
and an alley cat woke me a hundred times last night.
This morning I say, I forgive you. I forgive you,
alley cat, you are fine with me. Yowl, baby, yowl,
let it out, and I yowl with it. We yowl
and the neighbor yowls at his wife. Damn it, baby,
damn this, damn that, we aren't getting it right
no matter how hard we try, no matter how drunk we get,
how stupid we seem to ourselves, each other, and tonight
we are going to let it all out into the Halloween night.
In costume, in dress, in fishnet: these are our versions.
This may be a part of me you prefer. A part of me
you'd like to bend over, and the moon, too, is in
a version of itself. Costume. And my costume is a window
I look through, you look through, and I go out
for some candy. A candyland, the candyman can,
and I am myself on top of another self and I come home
with my selves and fuck myself, as it is too late now
for the trick-or-treaters. No little guys at my door.
No chickens, no heroes, no ghosts. But, they are still
out there. The vegetables walk the streets tonight:
this is the madness within us: this is the time to get it right.

SPIDER

A spider hangs over the dinnerplates, she looks
right in my bowls. The potatoes (or is it the meats?) intrigue.
I'm all here behind my nightclothes. Million filaments,
I must hang in her, too.

        Growing here, a partnership over rolls,
fellowship over wine. We cannot grow sleepy –
we've husbands to eat, and visions (what big catches
we'll be heavy with tonight). We climb to our corners
and wait.

How long? I ask. A minute or two? I ask and I ask.
I ask so hard I crack the room in two.
I crack the night in two. Two people together
in two. I wait for the spider at breakfast,
I wait for her at lunch. By dinner,

when she hasn't come, I know somewhere
she is full, rounded-out, her middle a little hill
too high to look over.

     We are together again
in our unseeing. But she,
she is luckier than I – rounded-out
by potatoes and rolls alone – and I wait the whole
broken night to tell her.

At breakfast I announce,
I've forgotten you, spider, I do not need you.
The toast quiets. The eggs stare back –
round and clean,
but stupidly.

BULB UNDER SNOW

Last Halloween my nephew was a dragon.
He refused to take his costume off, wore it for months,
dragging behind the long lump of tail.
Slept in it, even. The sparkles fell from the scales
in a trail where he walked, and he began, slowly, to stink.
No one believes he breathes fire, or that it was him
that set a little flame between his parents
that night in November when the first snow
of the season was softening upon the roof, and his parents
turned to each other, and what they found there, at last,
was good. Most people set reasonable explanations upon things,
sort things tangibly with nods and indeeds, all so sure,
and they are lucky, so I don't tell them
how the little tattered dragon in boots
breathed life into a yardful of angels in the January snows.
I wonder if it's the costume. And I constantly wonder
what I could be if I could just be, what I could hold to
as my nephew does as he does, as he sets
his little breaths upon things. He believes wholly
in his dragonhood. As I hold his little body
in my lap, his limp scales across my arm,
I try hard not to beg for his secret, but I almost
shake him off when I show him how deep I shiver.

WINTER GOSSAMERS

Today is run day, so I must run under the heavy mists,
through fog, through haze, water in both shoes, and I must
go soon, up the road and past the cattle, because this day,
as it grows grayer, shade-by-shade, will declare itself night
by noon. Why shouldn't it? Even the children do
what they want to. Laundry day, and they run with sheer
white sheets over their heads, around this little house
and through. Look at them, ghosts. They boo! And boo!
I'd sing them a lullaby, play hide-and-seek, but they are gone
before the one-two. I shouldn't have; I wouldn't have,
but I never would have made it to you. I come alone,
come clean, come running with my train of little boo-hoo's.
My mother said I should have been a nun.
My father might have said it too, but I went this way
and that, and to you, only for you to measure me, hand-by-
hand like they do the horses, right up from their horse
shoes to their shoulders. Maybe I measured
you, too, but this is what I really like: I measure the lawn;
I measure the stilted trees. I'd measure the blue bird,
but it flew, and my happiness, too, I measured it
against the stream, a lemon drop, a good poem in the pile
so it will be something I can get back to. Oh, the things we do
in winter. A hand shadow on the wall: a goose, a horse,
sheep in the meadow, cow in the corn. What time is it?
Already two? I must run, this way and that, just a little jog
up the road, not far, I'll make it back to you.
One foot in front of the other, each foot tied inside
its little wet shoe. Yes I will, I'll return, cold as a ghost,
but wet, alive, and maybe not quite as see-through.

THE MIDWIFE

Aren't I a stellar nurse this morning in my white gown?
You could call me friendly, almost. I have my gauges,
my switches – mimicries of control. And my patients,
they come and go. Around here, we call them
moods and I am never alone. I nurse their aftermaths:
little sadnesses that puke and spit on the white
floor. Hush, babies, I say, don't cry no more.

I entertain them (but what for?) – drink straight
from the faucet. Magnified in my ear: water against plates
(a little domestic downpour) and other things
are magnified this way (a midwife's attentiveness). Look,
my white gown! Am I marrying? The walls implore.
Only the little babies. I birth them, why shouldn't I?
(Others, we've decided, are really such bores.)

The babies are cold. Outside, the rawboned trees
are in their midwinter uproar. I scream,
but the patients ignore. I should leave them –
stupid and sore. I could, you know, I've these gauges,
switches – mimicries of control – but I am tired,
worn to the core. You'd agree, I'm sure,
that leaving tonight would silence them
like never before.

WINTER WEDDING WAITING

My man says he'll marry me
when he believes I trust him,
when I believe he wants no other.
I believe one morning I will wake
and the tulip bulbs I planted last fall
will have pushed up through my skin.
Look, I am a spring garden this morning!
Look, aren't I marriable? Well,
isn't this how it works: a bulb in the dirt,
a hope in the dark. He gave me a picture
taken in the 30s of thirteen men dressed
in gowns. A womanless wedding. I looked
at the picture while he folded laundry.
I looked at the picture while he cooked soup.
I looked at the picture while he set the dinner-
plates, and our cups runneth over. The dog
laps, laps, laps. Each of the men, man
& woman at once. Thirteen screams
from the picture: I am one! I am one!
I am one, yeah, well, Let *us* be one,
I scream across the dinnertable. I scream
myself awake from the banquet hall
of my sleep: I was there, it wasn't beautiful,
the room was full of ghosts in gowns.
A waltz, a bad country song, our great,
great grandmothers at the chicken dance,
flapping their wings viciously: fly away,
children, fly away while you can. The sky
is like this to me: a winter wedding waiting,
and I watch it behind you as we sup on our dinners.
Always a window behind you, always a door.
We are boyfriend and girlfriend, though boy and girl
no more. Your chest hair grows gray beneath
your shirt, fast as monkey grass, and, well, honey,

put your ear to my skin and tell me what is growing
there because in that dream the ghosts started
fucking the winter gardens, each of them horny
from their womanless wedding. Bulb in the dark,
hope in the dirt, and it wasn't just confetti
that flew, flew, flew from beneath their gowns.

Part Two:

Or Sit By the Door

Goodnight comb and goodnight brush.
Goodnight nobody.
Goodnight mush.

— Margaret Wise Brown

THE SWEETNESS (NO, THE SADNESS) OF A SUMMER STORM

My mother is hard of hearing –
a trait I did not inherit; I can hear for hundreds of miles.
Right now I hear my baby far away: her little whimper closes against the evening,
the door shuts with a click.
                                                              I am here
for work, two states away.
The hardest work, though,
is shooing away that old loneliness –
old dog. Oh, the ugly horns blow! (I am in the city; I hate the city.)
Weeks ago, in Helen, Georgia an accordionist told my husband that you must learn
the accordion young, to build muscle memory. I can hear my father playing
an accordion song – it stretches across this hotel
into me. The sweet, sad muscle memory of being alone.

Sad stories lose something upon a second telling – I only tell my mother
a few things, repeatable things. One thing I did not tell her:
months ago, after a tornado ripped through east Tennessee where we live
(where we drive the back roads
to put our baby asleep) they found a husband and wife in a wheat field,
still holding each other.
If I shut my eyes real tight I can stop the sound of the wheat
as it blows
and blows
and blows
and the horn blows and here I am. Here I am! There is nowhere I can go
that isn't my husband and my baby. The rug beneath my feet: warms me.

The storm comes down everywhere.

Only the middles of the wooden stairs are worn, there where my husband steps,
quietly so not to wake the baby. So quiet I can hear him

                                                                                            from
here.
Whisper this: does the land whimper beneath these streets?
I dream of tornadoes, simple as trees along the horizon.
They spin toward me and I watch as the red bricks beneath me loosen.

My husband right now is showering (we send each other these updates
because we are sweet and sad for each other). We are not together,
but we are together. The wheat grasses sing
of another family (another tornado)
in a trailer flying through these skies –
these right above me (how could that be?).
The trailer like a big, old rattle – my baby shakes hers and I can hear the pellets inside
sing their goodbyes:
I love you
I love you
I love you,
baby
(she stands by herself now).
She puts her head onto the floor to look at the world upside-down.
How sad she is going to be someday, for someone, something;
this spins toward her and I cannot stop it.
Stop it! I should say to my mother
when she tells me news of a boy drowning
except I don't say it (or did she not hear me?).
This news rattles so loud against me.

All of these noises –
all these terrible noises of the city –
just aren't loud enough right now.

KILLING HIM DIDN'T MAKE THE LOVE GO AWAY

Pecan

My husband sprays the gravel driveway with weed killer.
On the patchy places of our lawn we spread seed (I'm pretty
sure he'd be a happier man if the grass obeyed).
I think sometimes I'd be happier if I knew the names of the trees,
though I do know a few, the pecan because of its nut,
because there we hung a bird feeder, at the end of a cut limb,
(it hung too far, swayed too wildly, it's shadow so dark
upon our patchy, patchy lawn). We pronounce pecan differently.
When he sprays the driveway with weed killer I watch his sneakers
on the gravel. I watch the grasses and the grassless patches.
I watch the baby with her teeth small as grass seed
crawl toward our shoes so happily. Once, on the lawn,
she looked up into the leaves of the sweetgum tree and laughed.
On the roof of her little mouth was a leaf.

Tree-of-Heaven

On the west side of our house a forsythia bush grows,
and for a while, at its feet, a tree-of-heaven grew, too,
before we cut it out. At first we tried to save it,
but after yanking and ripping and hacking at it with the shovel,
it was too late. The forsythia is neater now,
prettier, as are the trimmed hedges, lawn, driveway.
I wonder about the relationship of the bushes we separated,
about the lady in the song who said killing her husband
didn't make the love go away. E.B. White said,
our approach to nature is to beat it into submission.
I feel sad about the tree, happy about our pretty yard,
happy about our love (would I be happier
if I knew the names of the flowers?). The rhododendrons
we pulled from the forest trail droop beneath the feeder.

Sweetgum

The first gift my husband ever gave me was a seedling.
After five years in a pot we finally planted it
beneath the feeder. The male cardinal comes for the seed.
The female waits in the thrush. I can name these two birds,
so easy to recognize. I know the sweetgum tree
because of its seeds (the sweetgum balls dirty our pretty yard).
Branch by branch, we cut the tree down, pile it
on the sidewalk for the city workers to haul away.
We hang ferns on the front porch. The flowers
sweetly fill the bed. My husband knows the names of the trees,
birds, flowers, even the grasses. I know a few of each.
I know how quickly storms come in spring.
The breezes pick up to a wind. The leaves spin.
We hurry to put the shovels away. Our baby,
she sits in the grass so happily as everything moves
around her. She waves, she laughs, she kicks her little feet,
yet she doesn't have words for any of this.

TRACTOR RACE

My father competed in a tractor race blindfolded,
his new wife behind him holding the reins.
It is easy to picture this – we've all seen a rider
atop a horse, or two people working together
to get to an end. My father and his new wife
did get to the end, they got there first and waited
for the other couples: the slower ones, the ones
a bit more careful, and some others – the drivers
a little misled. When my father and his new wife
stepped down from their tractor – their ribbons
lifting a little in the wind – the audience clapped,
and clapped, clapped long and hard, as we often
clap harder at what we cannot see. One couple
in the tractor race did not make it to the end.
The wife led her husband off the tracks, through
a fence, out a gate, between parked cars, and over
a hillside. The wife steered her husband far
from the clapping audience, far from the fair fields,
cameras, parents with their tickets and drinks.
As the couple disappeared behind the barns,
the couples in the audience turned away, some
covered the eyes of their children. Even now
they try not to think how the two of them
rode off, how they are out there now by the river
washing their feet and pinning each other
with ribbons of twigs, grasses, and fallen leaves.

LUMBER

For weeks I have been here, eating and putting on my shoes
one at a time, as if I may go out in them,
out in the street where the neighbor's dog sleeps.
Strange squeaking birds roar past my window, and lately
I've been thinking of having a baby (even in the middle
of all this danger). I must, and I must because I am getting old,
the thought of which spreads out in front of me like a lawn,
the streets two women in town walk down
with their babies strapped to their front-sides.
The babies like little beans are happiest then.
The blonde mother is pretty, she smiles at my husband,
and the young girls spend all summer in their swimsuits.
It is no wonder at all he calls the plastic playhouse
across the way a dollhouse. Dolls, dolls:
it is my deepest tendency to feel jealous of absolutely everything.
The tomatoes in the garden blush and ripen.

~

I run toward myself in my sleep crippled and old,
squeaking like a big strange bird (even awake
I do these things). That bird settles down upon me
so heavily I cannot see straight. My husband smiles
at me, but I cannot smile back. My face is as heavy
as lumber. My body, too – lumber.
The best thing you could do is build with me
and call me home, I say, and he does,
and he pulls out his drill gun, he fiddles for a screw.
I laugh every time he says caulk; he knows, simply,
I am happiest when we play, when we pretend, when we run.

~

In Georgia I met a boy with a syndrome that made his skin
stretch, his bones as soft as beans. Everyone took a turn
twisting his ear as if he were a wind-up toy. Are we all toys?

By 50 he'll be in a wheelchair. By 50 the boy next door will have
a belly round as the hillsides, but right now
he is filling up the dollhouse. Dolls and toys
and little boys – in a setting such as this I could be anything.

NEW MOTORCYCLE

My friend said she likes a man who looks like he could last
through the winter. She said this over Easter ham as it sat
split open, each of us with a slice on our plates, and sometimes
I pretend my man started his life when we met, and that I know
each of his winters, that there was no grief, sadness, other women.
Other times I watch him carry it all beautifully, pushing along
like a shiny hearse. At my grandfather's funeral my dad said
his dad's coffin was the same color of his new motorcycle.
He said this as he rubbed the coffin like he would have done
at the motorcycle shop, right beside my grandfather's feet,
and just like that grandpa rode off, revved up right there,
kicking up flowers, and burning through the rug.
The fat hung from the Easter ham in strings and chunks, and I fed
most of what was on my plate to the dog under the table.
I never really liked ham or meat or how I imagined animals
coming back alive inside my body and taking their revenge.
My mind takes revenge. The thieves take their revenge,
and the television sets, jewelry, the money from our wallets,
and I dreamed last night that I was my man as a little boy
protecting his family from thieves. A big him inside
a little him inside of me protecting me, protecting us, protecting
the dog protecting us, and I wonder if the dog thinks of the world
as a great bathroom. Sometimes I have to pull my car into the
shoulder
as the meat inside of me comes alive, galloping through my intestines,
roaring, kicking, and somewhere my grandfather
is doing a wheelie on the off-roads of heaven, hell,
or wherever he went all shiny and new like how my man
came to me, like how I imagined the Easter ham
as he zippered up his middle, lifted his sweet Easter head
and headed off the table and into the yard to roll in the sunshine
with the dogs. Right now I feel safe. The sun shall shine.
Spring has sprung and the buds have sent their stems through the
dirt.

My man and I, we've made it through the winter, and my father
who lives 800 miles south made it through a few weeks ago.
But my mother, well, she lives a thousand miles north,
and she keeps telling me I ought to buy a motorcycle. I don't know why.
I think sometimes she lives through me, vicariously. I think sometimes
she wants to ride off like grandpa. Galloping like a horse.
I think she wants to be shiny and new, wants to ride off past her bills,
her bad job, the yards in town on fire, right on
past her winter that's held her for years like a fist.

ADVENTURE, ADVENTURE, OR SIT BY THE DOOR

My husband tells me nice things, so I iron his shirts
while it rains outside. I'm careful around his buttons.
Careful what I say. Careful around our baby
scooting across this floor. How dangerous I am
with this iron, how dangerous this mouth.
Our baby has his eyes; she is like a little spy,
an investigator of all things. She is simply smarter
than anyone I know. This morning she got stuck
under the piano bench and cried. I cry most days
over smaller things, but not today, even when
the hot buttons burn me. Because today I feel close
to my husband, even when he is not here; we are closer
than these fibers flattening beneath this iron –
this iron that a few minutes ago the baby was reaching for.
Our baby moves across these wooden floors like a broom.
When I lift her, she is covered in dirt and dog hair
and little strings that have fallen from our clothes.
How slowly we unravel; you'd hardly notice
if you were in here. The rain falls and falls.
We are terribly alone, this baby and I and when
I lift her she flips in my arms like a little fish.
I've told you before, our house is like a boat –
we float here. The rainwater fills our yard,
our basement: I'd like to think I am saving this baby,
keeping her from harm. Some people have said
our baby is sweet enough to eat, they stretch toward
her with their hands and teeth, but these people,
they are not here, they are trapped outside by the rain.
I iron and she sweeps. For a little while it is easy
to forget just how much floor spreads out in front of us,
how many shirts are wickedly wrinkled, how many people
are out there in cars and boots, muddying up this town.

THE ROOF

It was years ago and my brother meant it
as a joke. He pointed across the dusty yard
to the 5000 sq. ft. barn with the rusty tin roof.
He said, *you must scrape the rust, prime it,
then paint*. He grinned, handed me a 3 inch
steel brush and a ladder.

On that roof I felt alive.
Sweat running down my nose, skin flaking
from the sun. A muscular masterpiece up a ladder.
On that roof my future filled with possibilities.

It's not like that now. I dissolve –
an Alka Seltzer bubbling in a glass, communion
tablet to a greasy spoon. Yesterday someone told me
I've probably been lied to my whole life.
This morning as I sit pondering this a goat appears.
I invite him in for breakfast, we talk
politics over coffee. *I hate politics,* I say.
The goat listens as he puffs,
puffs his cigarette.

I once floated off on the cigarette puff of my lover.
I floated over the aftermaths – train wrecks,
floods, leftovers from hurricanes: roofless houses.
I should have floated to the stars
while I still had a chance. I still thought it possible
then to be a star. No. I was in a hurry to get back.

Back, back
to the lover's lies. The wrong kind of lie.
Here I am a cow, lined behind
the ass of another cow. Waiting for the great
heifer. I stopped lifting
my head to the moon years ago.

I want my roof back. I want to sweat
and feel alive. I tell the goat how I finished
that roof, painted it blue. From an airplane
that roof looks like a swimming pool.
I am the swimmer. I tell him
I agree I've been lied to.
But I believe them less
than I believe my own lies. Look
in my eyes you can see my surrender.
I see myself as a ladybug
climbing the back-porch screen.
Through each and every square screaming
Save me! Save me!

THE SISTERS

My sister and I ate two ends of a sofa.
We munched until our munching
found us in the middle where we met
rubbing our bellies as one
both in and out of a long-length mirror.
We grinned, with fabric and stuffing,
little wedges of our lives sticking
from between our teeth.

With nothing left to sit on
and the wall offering nothing
but a large, tight mouth,
with our emptinesses ringing against each other
like a parade of dinner bells, we get
ourselves outdoors and stick our fingers
into the ground.

We grow there, our thirsts rooting
out from our fingertips, backsides
sticking upwards like hedgerows.

In the afternoon the landlady comes with her trimmer-
shears, trims off quite a large measure
of our backs and fronts and sides.
We laugh at each other for the better
half of an evening, enjoying
our new look and squarenesses, until,
misconceived by our own fun,
the neighbors click on their porchlights
to see what all the screaming is about.

HOUSE

A broken latch and the screen door catches
in the wind, again – the raised sail
of this stubborn old boat, this old docked boat
and I've got these silly oars out the window again.

House loves it when we play this game.
He's so old, I'm sort of keeping him alive –
all high, high-heeled, and lipsticked,
I drop my oars, fall to his floorboards.
He creaks! He's jealous! We are in love!
I picnic on his roof.

Indiscreetly over sandwiches, I watch
the neighbor-children play between
the bending dandelions. A tail-less cat
crosses the grass – a quaint cat, so surprising
the children shout, melancholy shouts,
selfish, little shouts
amongst these real, live goings-on.

LETTER AFTER THE CIRCUS

The ants carry their magnificent loads with such gentleness
across and into the dirt which, for the dirt (without means for movement)
must be the worst torture. And I think right now we are all

torturing each other. Daring Young Men on the Flying Trapeze.
Gentle Ponies. High Wire Daredevil. With such magnificence
in the world, it seems I would begin to believe something else.

Wind. Rain. All descriptions are masks. Sirens, right now,
screech through the air of this house. The gentle ponies were not
gentle at all. The rev-up of the daredevil highlighted a set

of invisible strings. Before you met me you believed you were
a good man. One morning I rose into the next act – naked, bed-warm –
toward the river and I became the river. Even with your worm,

bobbers, hooks, you could not get me back. Back to you.
I stomp my foot and the ants scatter. The river pulls at the shore.
The circus goat struggled in my grip. Accuracies become other
things.

I was your sky. Birds, my messages. What, again, did they tell you?
As I hovered there between you and the universe, who swallowed who?
Clouds – masks above trees, and everything looked like a reach for
me.

Sky became sky. River river. And as I watch the ants
haul away the bird seed, I wonder what it is that I have become.

FROST

On a morning after Easter, the cardinals, like red eggs
in dry branches, lift off. Leafless branches, and this is no place
to hide, I once said, alone, to tea, to saucer and cup.
Even the birds know it is better to be seen, but all along
I had it wrong. They're together; they fly. High, high,
and yesterday I felt high on Easter eggs and Easter ham.
Meat, potatoes, vegetables and rolls, rolls, roll
me into the grass that this morning looks sugared with frost.

Sugar in the grass, sugar in my tea, sugar,
thank you for what you have done for me (for seeing me).
So I worry about the garden, spinach, squash, peppers,
and I worry about my eggs, the mother I may someday be,
as I watch the house shadow creep toward the house.
Little taps of the dog's paws on the hardwood.
Little pats of little feet of little children that are not,
but someday may be. The sun moves over the field
and the field surrenders. I surrender: take me.

A man who wrote a book about the moon surrendered.
Gun to the head. His book had tractors, all sizes and shapes
of men, spinach that lived. Those men live as I remember them,
some so cold they could have killed me. Killing men,
killing frost, and, please don't take the vegetables. Don't
take me. Don't make me go back. Teapot, cup, saucer,
and a different man with a different gun, a man who had
nothing to do with books about moons, shot himself, too,
but lived. At this point I would rip the earth out trying
to hold on. Rip and hold, rip and hold, and the man who shot
himself and lived can no longer swallow, and it is the biggest
scar to bare, I think, the scar of wanting to die.

EVEN THE RADIO

Am I less of a woman than even the leaves?
The way my body keeps me in bed today.
The way my joints have taken on
new directions and terms for themselves.

I apologize, the hurricane carries
my father's name. And I, baby
of wind am confused by this stillness.
In here only the fruit flies show movement.

How quiet they are, not much louder
than dust and openly passionate
about the fruit. They are careless
of my ache, which is everywhere.

It seems even the radio struggles;
its song lags through my air.
Luckily the leftovers have been disposed of,
the plates dried and stacked, the sheets clean.
How long yesterday did I vacuum?

SATURDAY AFTERNOON REMODELING THE CAMPER

When I was young, one of my chores
was to fetch wood for the woodstove.
Often the pieces would freeze together,
so I would have to hammer them apart.
I was small, but the cold was big. The sound
was big, and it's still out there, waiting around
with the winter. Hammering. The fall
is here; the sound, I hear it now – it falls
into me as I sleep (as simply as leaves
falling into the grass). My husband and I
and our dog sleep piled together like logs.
Even in the light of the harvest moon,
I cannot tell what or who it is that tries
to hammer us apart. Small things chill me.
When my husband stands under the trees,
I cannot tell where he stops and the leaves
begin. We were working on the camper.
I was painting. He stooped with the welder.
He sturdies things – the camper, the trailer,
and I asked him to weld us together.
I held out my arms for him. I got down
on my knees and begged him, but I held
a paint brush in my hand (perhaps he thought
I was painting the camper's underside),
and the welder was loud, and the wind
was blowing through the trees, and the leaves
looked really pretty in the afternoon light.

I TOUCHED HER HAND AND IT FELT LIKE SNOW

The onions in my greasy skillet move in their juices. They spit.
I have a feeling they do not believe in anything
but their savory natures. Any smart woman might, from time to time,
take advice from an onion. And I do.
I put on rouge and make my way to the park.

I sit on a bench next to an old woman. Pantyhose
wrinkled at the foot. These sounds, she says, cushion me.
River, bird songs, cars passing, wind through leaves, foot-scuffs of passersby,
sirens – layers of tragedy and sweetness that remind her, she says,
of love.

                                                Goodness
, the old woman is beautiful. I think that the woman
is my mother and I almost say, Mother – the word sits on the edge
of me like the man on the edge of the bridge. Mother, mother, mother –
just wants to edge off into this woman. It wants to be true.

And doesn't the man?
He is no more himself today than he is
the river. A swig from a bottle. A contemplation. As if his body
has become to him something disposable
                                            and I love
him for that
and for everything because there is something in him that reminds me
of myself. A monument.

The mouth of the river is open. We all want to be swallowed, I think,
so I tell the woman I agree, though not entirely.
Similar noises, I explain, cushion me at night while in bed.

Through a cloud of blackness, I never know exactly
what I am looking at.

Which reminds me of how ghostly I've become —
falling into and out of and through myself. Only the body of another
(even as disposable as they are) could hinge me
into myself.

The day calculates,
makes her exchanges with night like cashiers changing shifts
at the station on 7th and Elm, and somewhere
a child is falling in love with a star.

As I make my way home I remember that I forgot
to tell the woman about the storm. Even then, I was alone.
The storm was heavy. I was a child. I had dropped
my red mitten in the snow. From the window
I watched the flakes which seemed as big as my little
fists and in only a few seconds, I remember,
those flakes had completely swallowed my mitten.

VALENTINE'S DAY

Well I've got a line, and you've got a pole
And I'll meet you at the fishin' hole

In a black morning not yet open I dress by dim light,
quietly and in layers, red sweater, red socks, and I think
how this is the good part of a old dream. The good part
of a bad dream I woke from, and last night, at the restaurant,
I told the man, who is asleep now in the other room,
the part of that dream where the little girl goes mad.
Mad into an adulthood where things don't equal out
or measure up and, hey, this isn't what I ordered,
I said, too, as the waitress brought the wrong fish.

The wrong fish at the end of the pole. Hatchery fish,
and bad fish. Some fish swim away, some we throw back –
not out of hate, or dislike, but some are best left to the universe.
Left to the loons because the loons are hungry.
The neighbors are hungry, and once, in an old house
on Poplar Street I threw a roast out the kitchen window.
The second floor window, and it hit the roof next door.
I imagined one neighbor asking the other, what was that?
A roast, and what else could it be because meat flies, and flies
fly around the meat, and the fishes fly as if to say,
catch me, catch me, catch me if you can. And you can,
mister man. You can and you have, I say to the morning,
as if that should open the morning up because I just can't wait.

The pole leans against the doorframe. The line is tight.
We will swim later in the fishing hole, swim and catch
our dinner. We will string up a clothesline and hang
our shirts and socks, and my red socks, tonight, through branches
of maple and pine, will look a little like small strung hearts.

WINTERING

I'm hardly in the mood to tell you little things
like how a cardinal spent most of his day
landing on my steps and looking in through my screen door
as if he was trying to tell me something.
He was so little; he must have only had a little to tell.

Whatever it was, I waited all day,
                                  and I came to believe
that someday winter would end (that the nudity
of the trees would stop embarrassing me!). Of course,
you say, winter will end,
but there's more.

Someone once said,
each cardinal is born to carry the red of the fallen rose,
and other birds do the same for leaves – if only
I could begin to see such grace in nudity. I project;
my body is wintering, and without a single bird
to carry the loss for me.

I am less lucky than the trees.
I am less lucky than the rosebush in front of me.
Let me tell you how I've watched the roses
fall all winter, how I've begged the cardinal, too,
        but the bushes won't speak
                the cardinal won't speak.

Winter is so damn quiet; it holds its beauty
in such small things.
I am not small at all; I am wintering.

THE WEIGHT AND WASHING UP OF THINGS

My friend bought a Singer sewing machine.
My Husqvarna waited in a barn for sixteen years —
how dirty it was,
its needle sharp as a thorn.

My friend & I sew together; our stitches run straight between us.

Hem

We sew in the dining room of our old house that sits on a quarter-
acre plot on the edge of town. Our yard is neat,
a perfect hem.

To the west lives Ruth Number One. When I met her, I tell my
friend,
she apologized for her face.
Ruth Number One cannot hear much of anything anymore. I tell her
things.
My words drop in the grasses at our ankles.

I'm not sure my friend can hear what I'm saying, either.
The Singer motor is loud. The cars zip past — up the hill
they modify their mufflers, smoke cigarettes, ping them in our yard.
The Husqvarna purrs.

Ruth Number One lives with her bald son.
My father, also bald, kept a ceramic golfer on his desk
with the sign: I may be bald, but I still have all my balls.
My friend laughs; her needle bounces.

Mornings, Ruth Number One blossoms from the house.
White Lily.
She sets her little black dog beneath the maple tree.

Her yard bursts with red poppies. Hydrangeas: blue.

My husband cooked Ruth Number One dinner.
My friend turns to my husband (he reads *Canterbury Tales*
in the adjoining room). What did you cook? She asks.
These two, they love to talk about meat.

I sew crookedly; I rip the stitch.

Needle

Ruth Number Two lives in the house to the south.
In her yard, an old trampoline, the poles are bent, broken.
A playhouse that stood high as the treetops long ago
now lies in the grass.

I want to build a fence between us, I tell my friend.
I want to dig holes, pound stakes. I push the machine's pedal
to the floor boards.
Burn rubber.
Sparks fly.
The engine roars.
I tear off above the house, houses, warehouses.

Thread

In a pretty house on a neighboring street lives Ruth Number Three.
One morning while walking I stopped
(she was having a yard sale).

I bought this fabric there, I say to my friend.

Can she hear me?

My bobbin runs from its thread.

I bought her nightgown.

I visited her yard sale three times. The second time Ruth Number Three told me to sit.
She showed me a picture of her two young sons.

She sent them to the mailbox one morning to wait for the school bus.
A car roared down the street, killed her two boys.

My friend listens.

Ruth Number Three's white hair fell. Snow.
The tarps beneath the yard sale tables unrolled

(everything in the yard covered with blue tarp).

I stand alone on the street

(the Ruths must be inside their houses).

(I hate how these days are threaded, pretty as they are,
with stitches tight as the cold).

IT WOULD BE QUIET

Watch her, Amber Rose, standing there between a field of wheat
and a field of corn, in a gully, a margin, with the weeds and
wildflowers.
Now she's gone. A storm from the west. Her baby left with her
mother.
I write this as my husband and baby back out of the yard,
shopping for me today, mother's day – like a birthday but better.
Days ago we left to camp with my father. The buds of the red
poppies
in the yard were green, and when we returned, the poppy
had already burst, its red petals dropped in the grasses.
No one took Amber Rose from the pretty fields. She hadn't
been standing among the wildflowers. She put her cigarette out
and climbed in a pickup. She rolled the window down,
let her hair blow. She's young. She left her baby.
Her mother was scared she wouldn't come back –
she even hung missing daughter signs on the light posts.
On the days when I have no laundry to wash,
my daughter stands under the empty clothesline with her arms up–
she dances with the clothes as she imagines them there.
While camping we walked to the lake to swim – it's May,
the water's still so cold. I looked up and saw my daughter
face-down on the surface of the water. The way water carries
sound, I know there wasn't a fisherman that didn't hear my scream,
didn't feel my fear climb through the pole. My husband pulled her
up –
coughing and crying. I would have drowned myself if I had lost her.
When we returned to the tent I hung her suit on the line
my husband had strung between the trees. Inside the tent,
we kissed that little, cold girl all over. If only our loving her in this
way
could hold her to us. When we lived across the street
from Amber Rose I was afraid my husband would grow to love her.
She's so pretty, so young. The second day we camped
my father and I floated across the lake in his kayak.
We paddled quickly to the middle, then stopped.

We watched a heron for a very long time. I thought of a story
I had read recently about a woman who bled from her skin every day.
She visited a wizard and the wizard told her he could make it stop,
but only if he could change her into an insect or animal.
She chose the butterfly. The heron flew so gracefully,
so close to the water, closing the difference between
swimming and flying. My husband told me how he was watching
a mother bird at the feeder and her baby just fluttered in the air behind her,
without the skill yet to land. My husband and baby back now
from the store – I can hear her little, bare feet
running across the wood floor. I read somewhere
that life is like a horseshoe – fat in the middle, open on both ends,
and hard all the way through. I know right now I've never been
happier. I know my skin is changing – sometimes I feel
see-through, a butterfly wing. There's something so clunky
about being human, something I feel I'm just not getting right.
Laundry swishes in the machine, and on sunny days I hang our clothes
on the line and watch as our shirts and pillowcases
breathe with wind and dream of our bodies so full of life
and love and hope and fear and sadness. The rain finally comes
after hours of promising. Tomorrow my good friend
will give birth to a little boy, and she's asked me to be there.
Today is the last day for her – you know what I mean by this.
I know how Amber Rose's mother feels. The fear.
Dread. The cold lake so still. Even the smallest movement
ripples the surface for miles.

ABOUT THE AUTHOR

Jan LaPerle (married name Matthews) is originally from a small town in northern New Hampshire, but currently lives in East Tennessee with her husband and poet, Clay, daughter, Winnie, and dog, Mortimer H. Matthews. She received her MFA from Southern Illinois University. She teaches English at Tusculum College

Made in the USA
Charleston, SC
15 February 2013